HOW
TO DRAW
MONSTER FOR KIDS 6- 8

THIS BOOK BELONGS TO:

_____

love

Dear readers,

We hope this message has been well received by you and that you are enjoying your literary journey with TinDiri2dy Publishing. We are committed to providing quality content that stimulates your imagination and enriches your coloring experience. To continue to strive for excellence, we kindly ask you to take a moment to share your thoughts through a valuable review on Amazon.

Your review is invaluable to us because it helps us understand your preferences, what works for you and areas where we can improve. By leaving a review, you not only contribute to TinDiri2dy Publishing, but also play a significant role in shaping the reading experience of other book enthusiasts.

We wish you an enjoyable coloring experience and look forward to your valuable feedback.

We extend our warmest greetings,

Introduction

Welcome to the exciting world of drawing! This step-by-step guide is designed especially for kids who are eager to explore their artistic side. Grab your pencils and let's embark on a creative adventure together!

1. Gather Your Supplies:

Before we begin, make sure you have all the tools you need. Grab some paper, a pencil or two, erasers, and your favorite coloring materials. Find a comfortable and well-lit space where you can let your imagination run wild.

2. Start with Simple Shapes:

Every drawing begins with basic shapes. Try drawing circles, squares, triangles, and rectangles. These shapes will serve as the building blocks for your more complex drawings. Experiment with combining them to create interesting forms.

3. Practice Lines and Strokes:

Become friends with your pencil! Practice drawing straight lines, curved lines, zigzags, and loops. This will help you gain control over your pencil and develop the fine motor skills needed for more intricate drawings.

4. Explore Colors:

Colors make drawings come to life! Experiment with different color combinations. Don't be afraid to try bold and bright colors or soft and subtle shades. The choice is yours!

5. Choose Your Favorite Subjects:

Think about what you love and what interests you. Whether it's animals, monsters, flowers, or imaginary worlds, pick a subject that sparks your creativity. This guide focuses on drawing monsters, but feel free to explore other themes too!

6. Follow Step-by-Step Instructions:

Now, let's dive into the main event - drawing monsters! Follow the step-by-step instructions provided in your guide. Take your time with each step, and don't worry if it's not perfect. Remember, every artist started with simple lines and shapes.

7. Add Your Own Touch:

Once you've mastered the basics, don't be afraid to add your own creative flair. Maybe your monster has extra-long arms or a funny hat. It's your drawing, so make it uniquely yours!

8. Practice, Practice, Practice:

Drawing is like any skill – the more you practice, the better you become. Set aside some time regularly to doodle, draw, and explore new ideas. The more you draw, the more confident you'll become.

9. Share Your Masterpieces:

Celebrate your achievements by sharing your drawings with friends and family. Their encouragement will motivate you to keep exploring your artistic abilities.

10. Have Fun!

Most importantly, have fun with your drawings. Let your creativity flow, and don't worry about making everything perfect. Drawing is about expressing yourself and enjoying the process.

Now, young artist, it's time to unleash your imagination and create some amazing art! Happy drawing!

Monsters Everywhere

Did you know that almost every culture in the world has its own version of monsters? From friendly to fearsome, monsters have been part of human imagination for centuries.

Have Fun!

1   2   3

4   5   6

How to Draw

1

2

3

4

5

6

Monster Anatomy

Monsters can have all sorts of body parts. Some might have three eyes, six legs, or tails that glow in the dark. The fun part is, you get to decide what your monster looks like!

Have Fun!

1   2   3

4   5   6

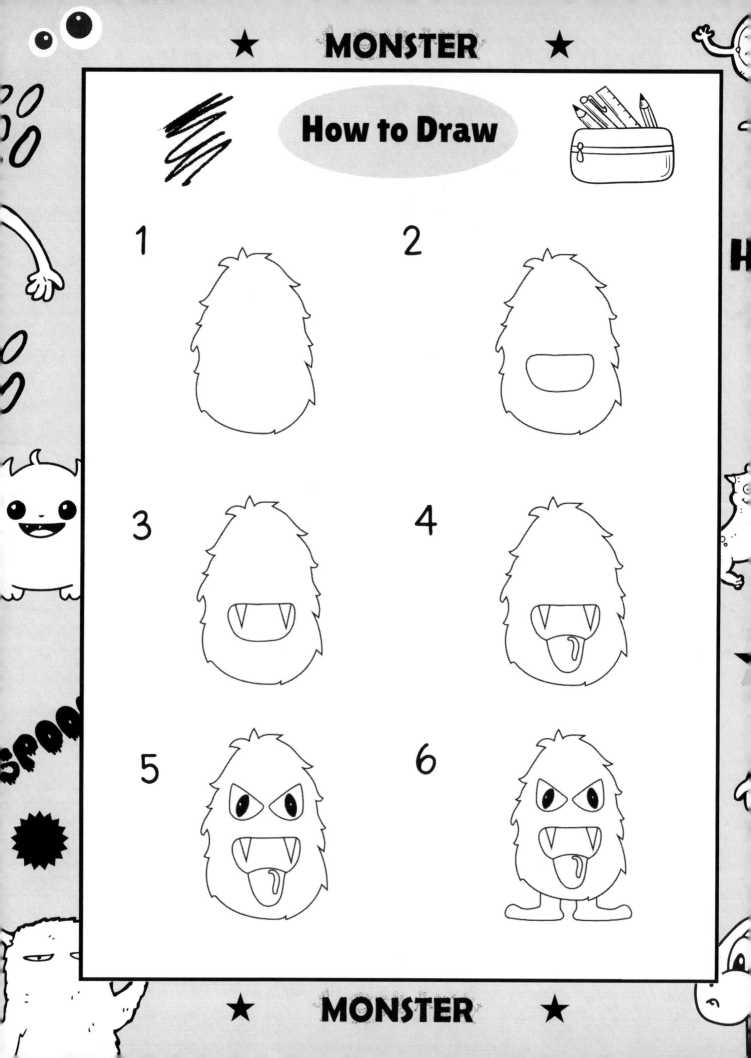

Monster Origins

The word "monster" comes from the Latin word "monstrum," meaning something that is marvelous and strange.

Have Fun!

1

2

3

4

5

6

Monster Hideouts

Monsters are said to live in all sorts of places, from under your bed to deep in the forest or even in the clouds.

Have Fun!

1

2

3

4

5

6

Monster Pets

In some stories, monsters can have pets too!
Imagine a dragon with a tiny monster as its
faithful companion.

Have Fun!

1

2

3

4

5

6

Monsters in History

Ancient maps used to have drawings of sea monsters in unexplored waters. People believed these monsters guarded the unknown parts of the world.

Have Fun!

1

2

3

4

5

6

How to Draw

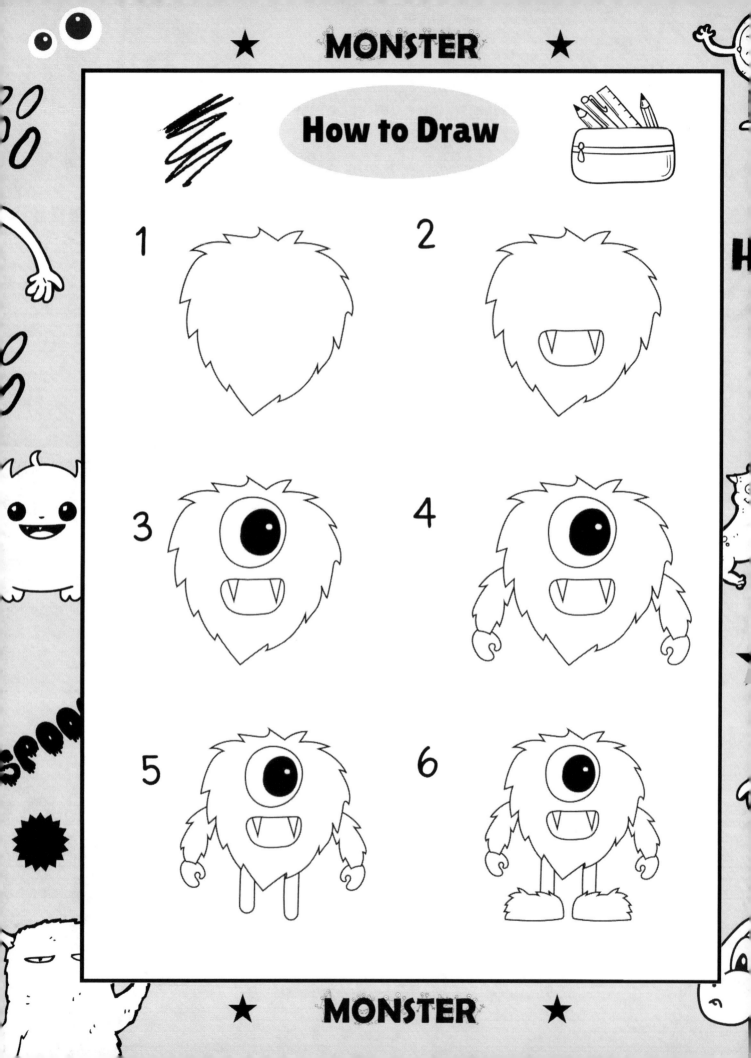

1

2

3

4

5

6

Monster Names

Monsters have cool names like Godzilla, Yeti, and Bigfoot. What name would you give to your monster friend?

Have Fun!

1   2   3

4   5   6

How to Draw

1

2

3

4

5

6

Monster Superpowers

Some monsters have special powers like flying, invisibility, or even the ability to change shape. What superpower would your monster have?

Have Fun!

1

2

3

4

5

6

Monster Parties

In some stories, monsters have parties when humans are not looking. Imagine a disco with dancing monsters!

Have Fun!

1

2

3

4

5

6

MONSTER ★

How to Draw

1
2
3
4
5
6

MONSTER ★

Monster Jobs

Monsters can have jobs too. Some might work as guardians, protecting hidden treasures, while others might be chefs cooking up magical recipes.

Have Fun!

1

2

3

4

5

6

Monster Families

Monsters can have families too! Imagine a big, friendly monster family living in a cozy cave.

Have Fun!

1

2

3

4

5

6

Monster Music

Monsters might have their own style of music. What do you think monster music sounds like?

Have Fun!

1

2

3

4

5

6

How to Draw

1

2

3

4

5

6

Monster Sports

Ever wondered if monsters play sports? Maybe they have a game of "hide and scare" or "dragon racing."

Have Fun!

1

2

3

4

5

6

How to Draw

1

2

3

4

5

6

Monster Languages

Monsters could have their own languages. Can you create a special language for your monster?

Have Fun!

1

2

3

4

5

6

How to Draw

1

2

3

4

5

6

Monster Holidays

Monsters might celebrate holidays too.
Imagine a monster Halloween with spooky
treats and friendly scares.

Have Fun!

1   2   3

4   5   6

How to Draw

1

2

3

4

5

6

Monster Hobbies

What do monsters do for fun? Maybe they collect shiny rocks, tell funny jokes, or have a contest for the silliest monster face.

Have Fun!

1

2

3

4

5

6

How to Draw

1

2

3

4

5

6

Monster Fashion

Monsters have their own sense of style. Picture a monster wearing a polka-dot cape or neon-colored fur!

Have Fun!

1   2   3

4   5   6

How to Draw

1

2

3

4

5

6

Monster Camouflage

Some monsters can blend into their surroundings. Imagine a monster that looks like a tree or a rock.

Have Fun!

1

2

3

4

5

6

Monster Friends

Monsters can be great friends. They might have a secret handshake or a special dance to greet each other.

Have Fun!

1

2

3

4

5

6

How to Draw

1

2

3

4

5

6

Monster Stories

Many famous stories feature monsters, like the friendly monsters in "Monsters, Inc." or the classic tale of the Loch Ness Monster.

Have Fun!

1   2   3

4   5   6

How to Draw

1

2

3

4

5

6

Monster Art

Monsters can be the perfect inspiration for art. Draw, paint, or sculpt your own monster masterpiece!

Have Fun!

1   2   3

4   5   6

Monster Taming

In some stories, brave kids become friends with monsters and even tame them. Would you be friends with a monster?

Have Fun!

1   2   3

4   5   6

How to Draw

1

2

3

4

5

6

Monster Legends

Some monsters become legendary, like the Kraken or the Phoenix. What kind of legendary monster would you create?

Have Fun!

1   2   3

4   5   6

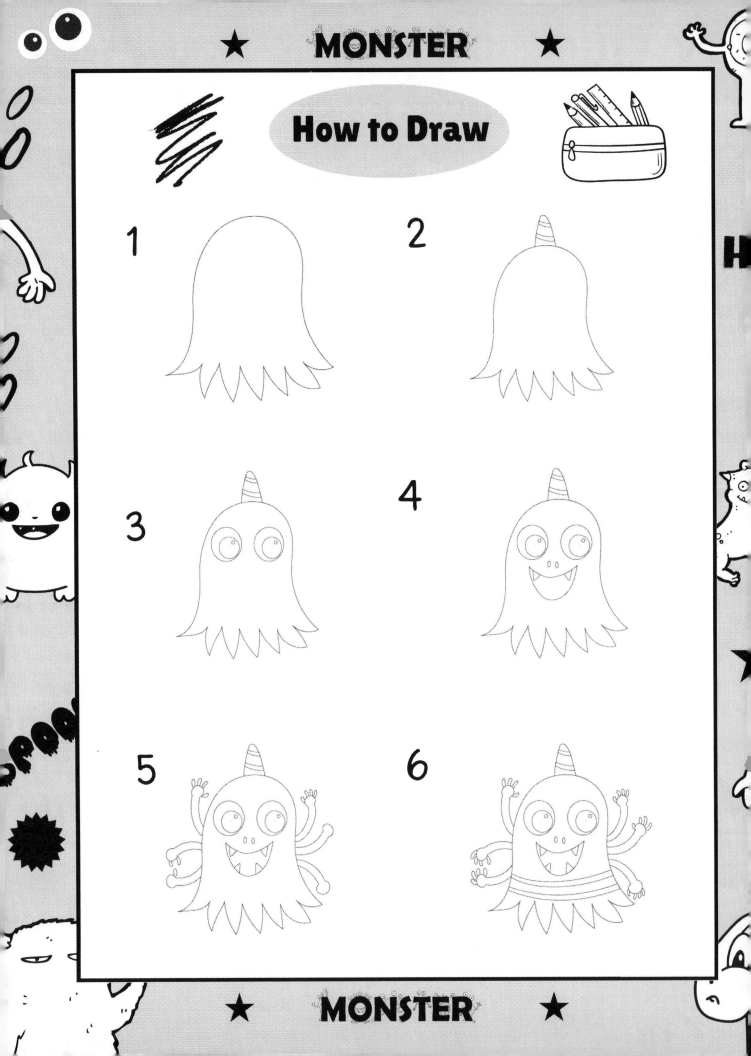

Monster Mirrors

Monsters might have their own special mirrors that show their true, friendly selves.

Have Fun!

1   2   3

4   5   6

How to Draw

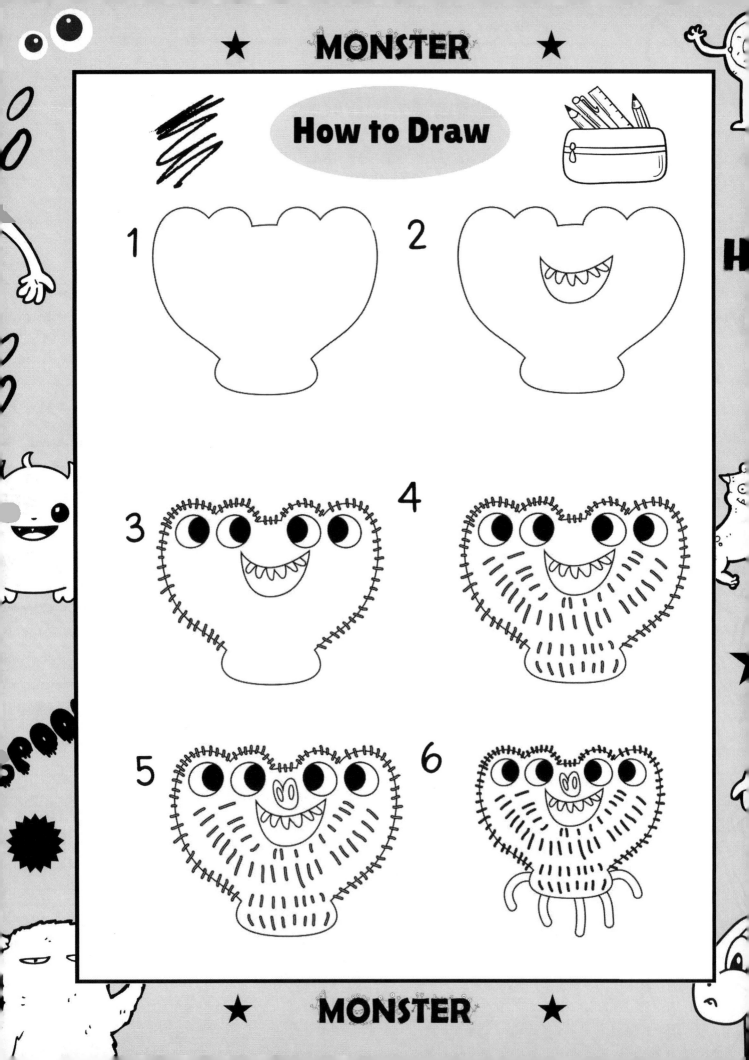

1

2

3

4

5

6

Monster Playtime

Monsters love to play games. Imagine a monster game of tag or hide-and-seek.

Have Fun!

1

2

3

4

5

6

Monster Dance Moves

Monsters could have cool dance moves. Picture a monster doing the "twist and roar."

Have Fun!

1

2

3

4

5

6

How to Draw

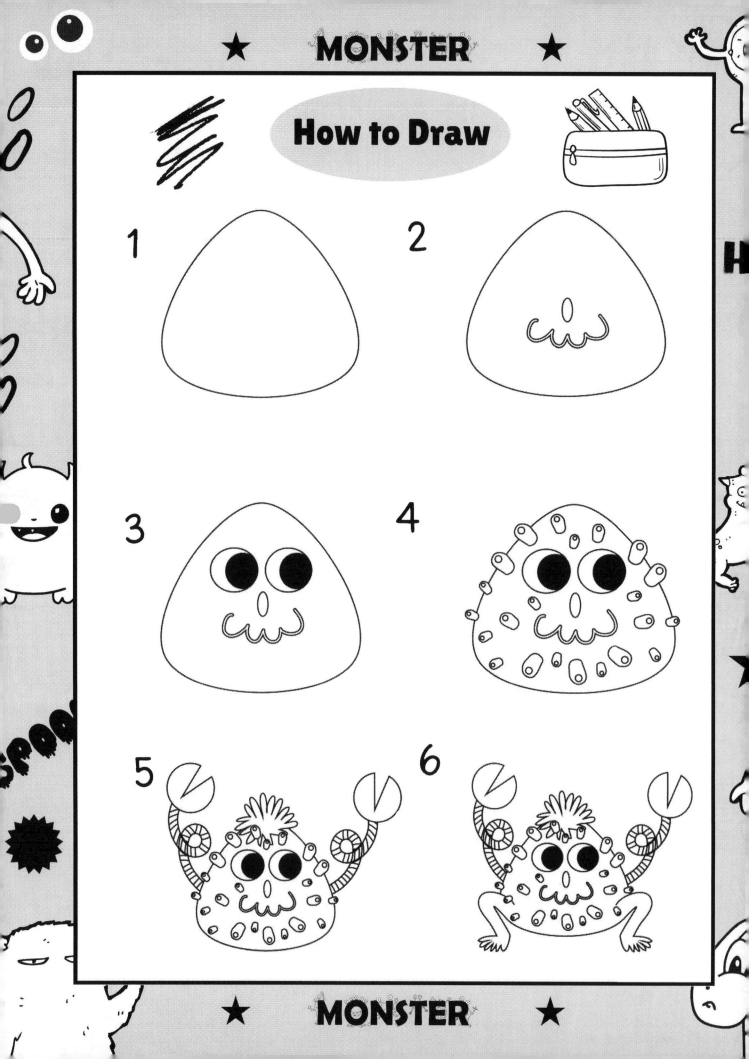

1

2

3

4

5

6

Monster Gardening

Monsters might have gardens filled with magical plants and colorful flowers.

Have Fun!

1   2   3

4   5   6

Monster Dreams

What do monsters dream about? Maybe they dream of flying through the clouds or having ice cream mountains.

Have Fun!

1   2   3

4   5   6

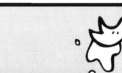

Monster Weather

Monsters might control the weather. Imagine a friendly monster creating rainbows on sunny days.

Have Fun!

1   2   3

4   5   6

Monster Inventions

Monsters are great inventors. Maybe they have a gadget that makes bubblegum clouds or a tickle ray.

Have Fun!

1   2   3

4   5   6

How to Draw

1

2

3

4

5

6

Monster Puzzles

Monsters love puzzles. Create a monster puzzle with hidden clues and treasure maps.

Have Fun!

1   2   3

4   5   6

Monster Sports Cars

Some monsters might have their own speedy vehicles. Imagine a monster zooming around in a turbo-charged wagon.

Have Fun!

1

2

3

4

5

6

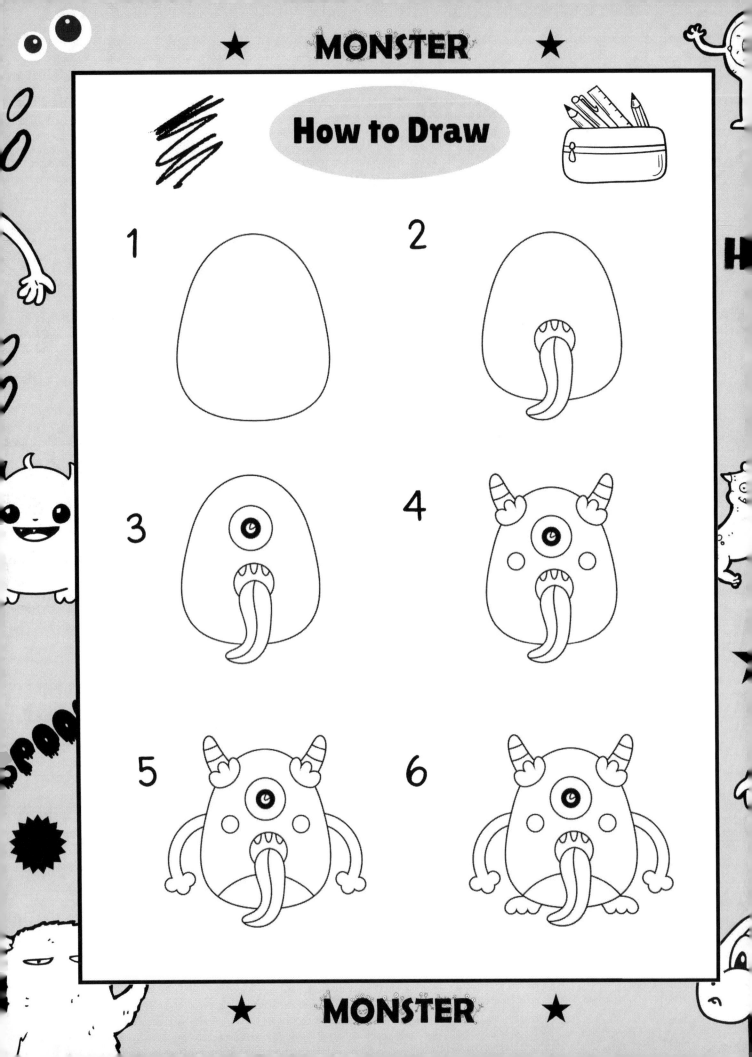

How to Draw

1

2

3

4

5

6

MONSTER

Monster Tea Parties

Monsters could have tea parties with magical
teas and snacks.

Have Fun!

1   2   3

4   5   6

Monster Art Galleries

Monsters might appreciate art too. Create an art gallery with monster masterpieces.

Have Fun!

1 2 3

4 5 6

How to Draw

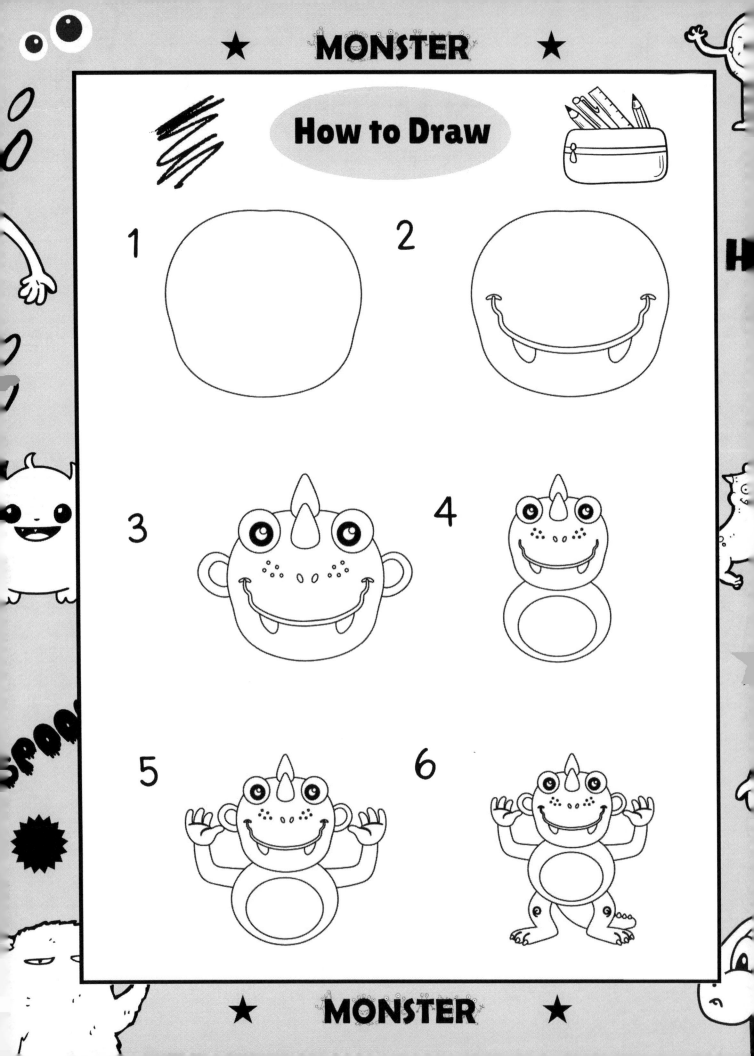

1

2

3

4

5

6

Monster Celebrations

Every year, monsters might have a big celebration where they invite friends from all around the world. What would your monster celebration look like?

Have Fun!

1

2

3

4

5

6

The Grand Finale of Monsterland

In the magical realm of Monsterland, where friendly monsters roamed and giggled, lived a little monster named Sparkle. Sparkle had a bright purple coat and a mischievous twinkle in her eyes.

One sunny day, an announcement echoed through Monsterland: "The Great Monster Book was coming to an end, and it was time for a grand finale celebration!"

All the monsters gathered in the Great Meadow, where the final pages of the book fluttered in the breeze. The wise old monster, Scribbler, declared, "It's time to close this chapter and begin a new one—a chapter filled with your own monster creations!"

Excitement filled the air as each monster was handed a blank canvas and colorful pens. The once-static pages now brimmed with possibilities.

As the monsters started drawing, they realized that this was their chance to bring to life the monsters of their dreams. Sparkle drew a monster with wings that sparkled like stars, while her friend, Giggles, created a monster that could tell the funniest jokes.

The moral of this monster tale: Every ending is a chance for a new beginning. The monsters of Monsterland discovered that they could create their adventures, bringing joy not only to themselves but also to the pages of the Great Monster Book. And so, Monsterland embraced the start of a grand drawing adventure, where every monster could contribute to the story, making each page a masterpiece of creativity and friendship.

Made in the USA
Coppell, TX
26 November 2023